THE GIRL I LEFT BEHIND ME

In the Middle of the West

T0347800

Neil Bartlett and Jessica Walker

THE GIRL I LEFT BEHIND ME

OBERON BOOKS
LONDON

WWW.OBERONBOOKS.COM

First published in 2011 by Oberon Books Ltd
521 Caledonian Road, London N7 9RH
Tel: +44 (0) 20 7607 3637 / Fax: +44 (0) 20 7607 3629
e-mail: info@oberonbooks.com
www.oberonbooks.com

Copyright © Neil Bartlett and Jessica Walker 2011

Neil Bartlett and Jessica Walker are hereby identified as authors of
this play in accordance with section 77 of the Copyright, Designs
and Patents Act 1988. The authors have asserted their moral
rights.

All rights whatsoever in this play are strictly reserved and
application for performance etc. should be made before
commencement of rehearsal to The Agency (London) Ltd., 24
Pottery Lane, Holland Park, London W11 4LZ; info@theagency.
co.uk. No performance may be given unless a licence has been
obtained, and no alterations may be made in the title or the text
of the play without the authors' prior written consent.

This book is sold subject to the condition that it shall not by way
of trade or otherwise be circulated without the publisher's consent
in any form of binding or cover or circulated electronically other
than that in which it is published and without a similar condition
including this condition being imposed on any subsequent
purchaser.

The publisher has made every effort to trace the copyright holders
of all images reprinted in this book. Acknowledgement is made
in all cases where the image source is available, but we would be
grateful for information about any images where sources could
not be traced.

A catalogue record for this book is available from the British
Library.

ISBN: 978-1-84943-197-2

Cover image by Fotofillia, 2010

CONTENTS

THE SHOW   8

THE SINGER   11

THE DIRECTOR   16

THE GIRL I LEFT BEHIND ME   22

NOTES ON THE AUTHORS   60

Vesta Tilley, date unknown

THE SHOW

The initial idea for *The Girl I Left Behind Me* came about as the result of a chance remark made in 2009 by Dominic Gray, the special projects director at Opera North in Leeds. As singer Jessica Walker stepped off the stage at the end of a concert of Tom Waits songs in a tuxedo and with slicked-back hair, he joked 'You remind me of Vesta Tilley'.

It's a name from British theatrical history still fondly remembered by only a few, and unheard-of by many more – but it was enough to kick-start a process of enquiry and collaboration which eventually produced the show whose script is printed here. The collaboration was between a singer who has never directed, and a director who can't sing. Here are our accounts of what happened next.

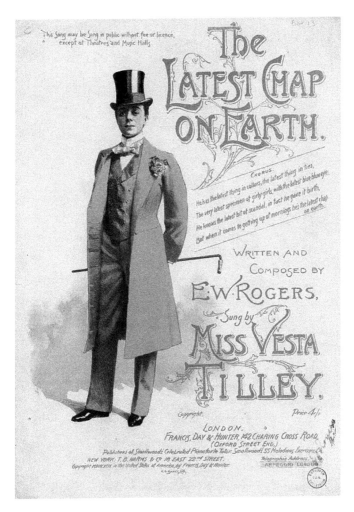

Show poster, 'The Latest Chap on Earth',
sung by Miss Vesta Tilley. c. 1899

Ella Shields, date unknown

THE SINGER

Dominic's comment aroused my curiosity; I knew that Tilley had been a male impersonator in the glory days of the British music hall, but had never actually seen a picture of her. Having sourced some images on the internet, I found that staring back at me was a crop-haired, small-faced and sharply-suited woman who looked remarkably like the stage persona that I had created for the Waits tour. While I was already aware that the look I had adopted was far from original, I had vaguely assumed this particular style of female stage cross-dressing was derived from Marlene Dietrich's infamous white-tie-and-tails number in the film *Morocco* in 1930. Through further reading, however, I discovered that the first singing male impersonators went back much earlier than that. In fact, as early as the 1860's one Annie Hindle – a woman who was as happy to be called *sir* as *madam* – was already wowing audiences in America by singing in full male costume. And Vesta herself, it turned out, though certainly iconic, was far from being a theatrical rule-breaker; indeed, she was one of the least daring of the male impersonators, living and performing as she did at a time when to be 'mannish' became openly associated with women's suffrage, not to mention the murky world of the sexual invert. It was the true pioneers of the form – Annie Hindle and Ella Wesner most particularly – who challenged social convention, spending periods of time dressed as and identifying as men offstage as well as on, and even 'marrying' other women. As early as 1888, I found, Wesner was dragged up as a man and singing, 'Lovely woman was made to be loved, to be fondled and courted and kissed; and all those who've never made love to a girl, well, they don't know the fun they have missed' – a fact which made my 2009 performances of a few Tom Waits songs wearing a tux rather less daring than I had previously imagined. I began to ask myself what motivated a woman, as far back as the late 1860's, to dress up as a man to earn her living on the stage. To whom did she wish to appeal, and to whom did she *actually* appeal? Was she dressing as a man on stage because it was her only opportunity to express a certain aspect of her personality, or was she simply dressing in a way that would gain maximum impact and therefore maximum financial reward?

I took these questions to Dominic Gray, as the fledgling thoughts for a piece about the male impersonators, and he immediately suggested that theatre director and author Neil Bartlett was the man to help realise my ideas. In our first meeting, Neil made the prescient observation that actually what we were going to be looking at in the piece was not why Annie, Vesta and Ella felt the need to put on trousers, but why *I* wanted to dress as a man when I sang on stage, a point that I chose, initially, to dismiss as too unsettling. When (for instance) I played a boy role in opera like Cherubino in *The Marriage of Figaro*, *I* had never been a consideration, because *I* was being someone else, on a stage shared with colleagues. The male impersonators, however, who were plying their trade at exactly the same time as their operatic counterparts, were standing on stage alone, in a self-created persona, rather than behind the mask that an operatic role provided. Where opera had hitherto afforded me the opportunity to cross-dress without ever questioning why I was doing so, it was immediately evident that a solo show, the subject for which I had chosen myself, was going to make me question what, or who, this trouser-wearing 'I' was. It became clear in our very first conversations about the piece that for a show about the now-dead male impersonators of the British Music Hall and the American Variety and Burlesque houses to be worth doing in 2010, it would have to be a contemporary reflection on their art – and one in which my personal relationship with the material would be central. Consequently, the narrator persona we developed together through the devising process – a solitary figure who told the stories about these remarkable women, and then sang their songs – became pretty close to a version of myself. S/he often spoke in the first person, and sometimes even forgot altogether that s/he was actually meant to be talking about somebody else. The words Neil gave me, together with his sensitive and skilful direction, drew out a swagger and flirtatiousness in my cross-dressed persona, and,

Francis, Day & Hunter

Nº1268 SIXPENNY POPULAR EDITION. (NO DISCOUNT ALLOWED)

OH, THE BAA-BAA-BAA-LAMBS!
(WAGGING THEIR TAILS BEHIND.)

WRITTEN AND COMPOSED
by
William Hargreaves
AND
Fred Godfrey.

Sung by
MISS ELLA SHIELDS.

The Music Hall Singing Rights of this Song are Reserved. Application for Theatre Singing Rights should be made to the Publishers. All other Performing Rights are controlled by the Performing Right Society Limited

Copyright

LONDON:
FRANCIS, DAY & HUNTER,
138-140, CHARING CROSS ROAD, W.C.
NEW YORK:
T. B. HARMS & FRANCIS, DAY & HUNTER, INC., 62-64, WEST 45TH STREET
Copyright MCMXV in the United States of America by Francis, Day & Hunter

Show poster, 'Oh, the Baa-Baa-Baa-Lambs!',
sung by Miss Ella Shields, date unknown

Miss Hetty King, date unknown

if you like, provided me with the safety net to be a little bit dangerous.

The logistics of how to move between the narrator, the ladies themselves and the characters taken on by them in their songs (not to mention where *I* fitted in to all that) could have been sticky, but because the devising process began with the selection of the songs and the hammering out of a draft running order – which Neil insisted should be the starting point – we had a firm structure within which to unravel, play with and then reconfigure both my speaking and singing voices. Far from being daunting, the rehearsals were in fact full of pleasure. The songs we had chosen, ranging from well-known numbers like *After the Ball* to nineteenth-century obscurities like *Down by the Old Mill Stream*, gave us a huge emotional and physical range to explore – not to mention lots of laughs. Luckily for us, we had the talents of our colleague, MD and accompanist Jim Holmes to draw upon; his ability to transpose and rearrange on the spot and to use the piano, in effect, as another character in the show, with witty instrumental interjections, created both texture and humour along the way.

Jessica Walker, 2011

THE DIRECTOR

One of my favourite ways of working in the theatre is to create a text with a voice in my head – to be working not in the abstract, but with and for a particular performer, one who intrigues and inspires me. That's why I eagerly accepted the chance to work on this project. Moreover, the solo performance is a form I love, and know well; its directness, its economy of means and its potential for direct contact with an audience are all cornerstones of my practice as a theatre-maker. The idea that 'I' can be both a stage persona and a person is crucial to my conception of what a performer is.

Moreover, I am no stranger to sartorial misbehaviour. My younger self quite often wore queer drag, and over the years I have often used both queer and theatre drag in my work, both male-to-female (as in my 1989 music-theatre piece *Sarrasine,* or in my own solo performance piece *A Vision of Love Revealed in Sleep*) and female-to-male (as in my productions of *Twelfth Night* for the Royal Shakespeare Company and for the Goodman in Chicago, in both of which actresses in trousers and moustaches turned the tables on anyone thinking that only boys should be allowed to dress up to do Shakespeare). I find cross-dressing on stage beautiful, funny, transgressive – and incredibly useful. It seduces and intrigues an audience straightaway. It immediately foregrounds both the vulnerability and the strength of the performer. It promises the audience some kind of transformation.

I also love the world of the music-hall – its architecture, its songs, its now-vanished audience, its glamour, its ability to make true stars out of the unlikeliest of performers. For me, it is space for dreaming in. And I believe passionately in reclaiming voices which have been written out of history – because they were too unlikely, too queer or too womanly. Like Jessica, I had heard of some of the British trouser-wearers, but like her I was amazed and delighted to discover the earlier and more radical pioneers of their art. I hope we have done them proud.

A word about the script. Solo performance is notoriously hard to transcribe, because so much of it depends on

Miss Gladys Bentley, date unknown

the tone of voice. This problem is compounded when so much of the show in question is sung. To this end, I have included indications of how Jess handled the material where appropriate, and sketched in some of the gestures of my staging where it seems helpful rather than prescriptive to do. I very much hope other women will perform this show, and I know they will find their own ways of staging it, their own voices, and their own ways of making these wonderful songs come alive again.

Neil Bartlett, 2011

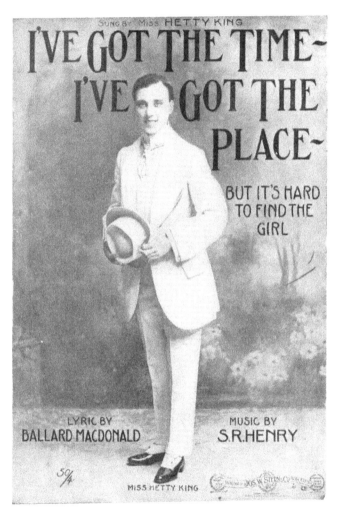

Show poster, 'I've Got the Time, I've Got the Place',
sung by Miss Hetty King, c. 1919

ACKNOWLEDGEMENTS

Thanks go to Dominic Gray at Opera North for commissioning the show, and to Dr Gillian Rodger for the generous supply of historical information.

The Girl I Left Behind Me

Devised by Neil Bartlett and Jessica Walker.

Commissioned by Opera North; originally performed by Jessica Walker, with James Holmes at the piano, in a staging by Neil Bartlett.

First performance 15th May 2010, in the Howard Assembly Room at Opera North in Leeds.

THE SONGS USED IN THE SHOW ARE

I'm the Idol of the Girls, Lyle/Murray/Hilbury, 1908

I Love the Ladies, Schwartz/Clarke, 1914

Jolly Good Luck to the Girl Who Loves a Sailor, Lyle/Leigh, 1907

Angels Without Wings, G. Dance, c. 1900

Don't Put Your Foot on a Man When He's Down, C. Vivian, c. 1870

Down by the Old Mill Stream, W. Wilson, 1875

Why Did I Kiss That Girl?, King/Henderson/Brown, 1924

Following in Father's Footsteps, E.W. Rogers, 1902

I'm Sowing All My Wild Oats, Lyle/Mellor, 1908

Hi, Waiter, J.F. Mitchell, 1888

I've Got the Time, I've Got the Place, Henry/Macdonald, 1910

Burlington Bertie from Bow, W. Hargreaves, 1915

Baby Won't You Please Come Home, Warfield/Williams, 1919

The Girl I Left Behind Me, S. Lover, 1866

After the Ball, C.K. Harris, 1892

THE TWO OPERATIC EXCERPTS USED IN THE SHOW ARE

Cherubino's Aria in Act II of 'Le Nozze di Figaro'
by Mozart

Octavian's Aria in Act I of 'Der Rosenkavalier'
by Richard Strauss

Jessica Walker, image by Fotofillia, 2010

A hatstand with a few hats, a table with a few props, a microphone in a spotlight – and a grand piano.

The house lights go down.

A piano player enters, bows as if he was performing in a very grand theatre, and starts to play.

OVERTURE
A sometimes jaunty, sometimes sentimental medley of the tunes to come. The last item in the overture is an instrumental chorus of 'After the Ball'.

A woman – immaculately dressed in white tie, trousers and tails, with scarlet lipstick and cropped hair – enters.

She looks at the audience. She stops by the hatstand and rearranges one of her hats, then lingers at the props table next to the microphone, lightly touching a couple of singularly male items – a cigar, an ashtray, a cane.

She speaks into the microphone. What she says is lightly punctuated by the pianist with chords that take us gently towards the next piece of music – sometimes gentle, sometimes melodramatic. They are indicated simply in the text by an **X**.

Good evening. Very early in my career, I realised that when I'm singing...I don't have to behave.

In fact, you might say that I make my living doing things I would never do – **X**

Saying things *I* would never say – **X**

And wearing things I would *never* wear... **X**

This evening, I would like to share with you sixteen and a half songs made famous by some outstanding pioneers of womanly misbehaviour – some of them famous; **X**

Some, infamous; **X**

Some fabulously successful – and some...obscure. **X**

Famous or infamous, handsome or petite, these Ladies had one thing in common; they were all *Male*

Impersonators – that is, they were *Ladies* who sang while dressed as *Gents*. *(She indicates her own costume.)* From head...to toe...

But...whatever they wore, whatever they said or did, these women always sang in their own voices – which meant that no one was ever fooled, or even meant to be fooled, by their act; **X**

which meant that it was all alright, because at the end of the evening, everything could go back to being just how it was meant to be in the first place, both onstage

X

and off; **X**

which meant, perhaps, that they didn't really mean what they were singing, if you see what I mean... **X**

Or...which meant – perhaps – that they were just ladies who

Like Post-women **X**

    Or like Bus-drivers **X**

        Or like *me*...prefer to work...in trousers. **X**

The piano begins a jaunty vamp under.

She picks up a walking cane from the table.

So, if you're sitting uncomfortably, I'll begin. This first number is an iconic little ditty made popular by the most successful trouser-wearer of them all. Born in poverty in 1864, Matilda Powles was rechristened the Great Little Tilley at the age of eight when her father dragged her up in evening dress and put her in the act – and then hastily rechristened again because she looked so convincing that some people thought she actually was a boy, which would have been...confusing – so, *Miss* Vesta Tilley she became, and she never...looked...back.

She plucks a top hat off the hat stand during the musical intro, and strikes a pose with her back to audience. She turns – and sings off-mike, in character as a cocksure young man – dapper, suave, flirting with the girls in the audience…

I'M THE IDOL OF THE GIRLS

I meet no end of nice girls, and 'pon my word, at times

I feel quite bashful when they say they love me;

It seems that I'm a magnet that attracts them, as it were –

There's no resisting me when I'm about;

In my dress I follow fashion, ev'rything's immaculate;

They cry, 'Why here comes Charlie, he's the Johnnies' fashion-plate!'

The girls they say they'd die for me – in fact the dark ones do;

My fav'rite colour's gold you see – that's why they change the hue…

I'm the Idol of the Girls; I'm the Idol of the Girls;

Fellows come along but they soon go, for they've got no show with the Girls!

I'm the Idol of the Girls – love their dainty little curls –

There'll be trouble if the wife finds out I'm the Idol of the Girls!!

Since I can first remember, it's always been the same –

I seem to have the knack of pleasing ladies.

When I was quite a youngster they would hold me in their arms;

Now I'm grown up they seem to like it more…

I often think when all these girls they follow me about,

There's must be lots of chappies out there have to go without;

The girls will sit upon my knee; they won't sit on a chair –

My valet has an awful job to keep the creases there…

I…

She suddenly jumps out of character.

27

…'m sure I'm not the only one who's thinking; hang on a minute;

'I seem to have the knack of pleasing ladies.'

In trousers? With short hair? In public? Was that allowed? Indeed it was. And not just in London – where by 1903 Miss Vesta was slipping £1000 a week into the pockets of her impeccably well-cut and apparently innuendo-proof trousers – beneath which, by the way, she wore male underwear; oh no – it was all the rage across the Atlantic too; oh yes –

'Meanwhile, in America'

She swaps her top-hat and evening cane for a straw boater and picks up a walking cane – and swings into a new character – another young man, but brasher and louder.

I LOVE THE LADIES

Young Johnny Dunn, was Twenty-one

He liked to dance in each cafe.

He liked the ladies – so they say, that's why he danced in each cafe.

His daddy's got, an awful lot, which makes it soft for little Dunn,

When he said 'Go to work, my son!',

Johnny said 'I'm having too much fun…'

She slips into a cake-walk.

I love the ladies, I love the ladies, I love to be among the girls.

And when it's five o'clock and tea is set, I like to have my tea with some brunette.

I love the ladies, I love the ladies, and in the good old Summer-time,

When I'm in swimmin', I love the women, for they make the swimming so fine.

When I'm in London, Paris, or old Vienna, or any other town,

I feel so homesick, homesick, unless I'm hearing the rustle of a gown.

I love the ladies, I love the ladies, I love the small ones, tall ones,

God bless 'em, the world can't twirl around without a beautiful girl,

The world can't twirl around without a beautiful girl.

'I love the wimmin'… 'I love the ladies' … 'I'm the Idol of the Girls'…I detect a theme emerging.

The girl in this case was one Miss Florenze Tempest – who with her sister, Miss Louise Sunshine, performed a double-act billed as 'Tempest and Sunshine' – with Lou as the Lady and Flo, always, as the Gent. They were not a success on the halls – so not a success, in fact, that they were forced to seek employment on the legitimate stage…

The hat and cane are regretfully discarded. She picks up soldier and sailor hats, and moves back onto the microphone.

So…just what was it that made a woman in trousers so modern, so appealing – and to whom? Was these performers' secret that they had a dirty little secret? Not at all; there was nothing secret about it – they performed in the most respectable of circumstances. *(The pianist strikes up an intro.)* Vesta Tilley starred in several Royal Command performances (though Queen Mary was said to have politely averted the royal eyes when the trousers came on stage…) – and when she made her farewell performance at the London Coliseum in 1920 (having married a man so rich she never needed to work again), she topped the bill with the 'patriotic' song she had sung throughout the First World War on Government Recruiting drives…

JOLLY GOOD LUCK TO THE GIRL WHO LOVES A SOLDIER

She puts the soldier hat on and salutes.

Jolly good luck to the girl who loves a soldier

Girls, have you been there?

You know we military men, always do our duty everywhere...

Or, if she had been playing Portsmouth that night –

She puts the sailor hat on and strikes a nautical pose.

JOLLY GOOD LUCK TO THE GIRL WHO LOVES A SAILOR

Jolly good luck to the girl who loves a sailor

Real good boys are we.

Girls, if you want to love a sailor you can all love me.

(With heavy irony.) – See, no dirt at all... *(Removes sailor hat.)* especially not on the stage of the Royal Opera House, where the hit show of 1913 opened with another lady in trousers – this time impersonating a teenage boy in pyjamas – climbing out of another lady's bed...

The pianist floats a phrase by Strauss...

She sings as if to a female-lover.

An older woman's bed...

OCTAVIAN

Wie Du warst

Wie Du bist.

Das weiss niemand, das ahnt Keiner...

The boy's name is Octavian, he's seventeen, and those are the opening words of Strauss's *Der Rosenkavalier*. Of course, in the Opera House, the audience – that'll be you – could always claim that they didn't know what was going on, because they didn't understand what the lady in trousers was saying – especially when she was in an older woman's bedroom and having some decidedly randy thoughts…as she was once again *(Removing dinner jacket.)* in a show that has rarely left the London stage ever since opening at the Opera House in the summer season of 1814…

Changing her body language yet again – into that of a gawky, randy teenage. The piano strikes up with some Mozart, and she begins to sing.

CHERUBINO

Sospiro e gemo senza voler…

(As if worried that the audience isn't getting this, she stops – and talks to the pianist.) – Sorry – sorry – I think they're a bit confused – but since we're not in the Opera House, I think I might take this opportunity to let the Ladies and Gentlemen know exactly what this particular lady in trousers is saying – as Cherubino, in Act Two of Mozart's *The Marriage of Figaro*; what she – I mean he – I mean she – oh you know what I mean – is saying is this:

(On mike.) I'm sighing and moaning, although I know I shouldn't…

(Off mike.) …Senza voler. Palpito e tremo, senza saper

(On mike.) My heart's beating thirteen to the dozen, and I don't know why…

(Off mike.) Non trovo pace, notte ne di, ma pur mi piace…

(On mike.) I can't help it – I'm at it night and day. But I like it…

(Off mike.) Languir cosi

(On mike.) I like....relaxing. So, ladies, you look like you know what it feels like. Tell me – is this the real thing?

(Off mike.) Voi che sapete che cosa e amor

Donne vedete s'io l'ho nel cor

...Of course, the lady in question could always respond to any accusations of impropriety by claiming

'But that wasn't me singing those words; I was in character!'

A defence I shall not hesitate to avail myself of should it become necessary...

(Back on mike.) Perhaps that's why, in the music hall, where every act was introduced with the singer's name, the songs often began in the third person , with an announcement of the *character's* name – Tom, Dick, Harry; Johnny **X** Charlie **X** Bertie **X** to make sure everyone knew that **this isn't me** – I mean, *wasn't her* – singing – and of course every song had its own ... *(Piano flourish as she retrieves dinner jacket.)* ...costume and *(Piano flourish as she removes cigarette from cigarette case.)* ...prop that said – most emphatically – this isn't me; I'm just... playing... *(Saucily holding the cigarette erect .)* a part.

Which still begs the question; is this

Suggestion? **X**

A new pose with each chord...

Or is it... Provocation? **X**

Is it Substitution...? **X**

She holds the cigarette jutting out saucily from her trouser-clad groin.

Or even...*(Putting the cigarette in mouth.)* Identification...

If the performer is a mirror, whose sex – whose sexiness – is 'she' actually reflecting, when 'she' is 'carrying himself' like a 'he'? Well *(Putting on white gloves and talking with the cigarette in her mouth.)*…to judge from the rather rancid tone of many of these numbers, 'he' was telling the men in the audience how sexy they were… **X** while at the same time telling the women in the audience…how sexy they were **X** … to the men sitting next to them **X** … Listen –

ANGELS WITHOUT WINGS

The ladies – heaven bless them – now we love them, ev'ry one

We praise them and we toast them o'er our wine.

We laud their many virtues and we sound their many deeds

And call them darling angels so divine.

– But, maybe at the time the little husseys are at home

Pencilling their eyebrows without shame.

Their blushes as divine are ten to one carmine

And still we call them angels all the same –

Angels, angels, angels without wings.

Simple, very simple, very pious little things.

Angels, angels, angels all about.

Like us men, they're angels when they're not found out...

Getting up from chair.

Angels, angels, angels without wings.

Simple, very simple, very pious little things.

Angels, angels, angels all about.

Like us men, they're angels when they're not found out.

Stubs out cigarette.

– That song was made famous by Miss Hetty King, who after Vesta Tilley was the most famous of the British male impersonators... Hetty King, who married three times, and of whom it was said when she took her act to New York *(On mike.)* 'Miss King is so real-looking a girl-chap that she might saunter down Fifth Avenue by broad daylight without raising any suspicion of sexual fraud...' Well that's alright then... Hetty was still singing that song at the very end of her career, in her eighties... and still saying, in an interview given in 1972, 'there is nothing more objectionable to me – and I don't care who I offend by saying it – than a mannish woman...'

Thank you, Hetty.

– Back in the early days, things were very different. I'd like you to now meet a woman called Annie Hindle – 'Hindle – The Apollo Belvedere of the Vaudeville Stage' – **X** – note, no 'Miss' for her... Back in 1864 Annie was the very first woman to specialise in male impersonation on the halls. Born in Hertfordshire, she first sang in men's clothes as a joke **X** – then went to America and became a star **X**... *(Striding across stage.)* Annie is reputed to have occasionally worn a moustache and stubble between performances – and is on record as saying that she didn't care whether her fan mail came addressed to 'Madam' or 'Sir' **X** Like Hetty, she got through three husbands **X** ...the last of whom was... a wife **X**... Annie was a pioneer, and she sang like one – when she put on her trousers , Annie raised her voice in songs about things that women *really* weren't supposed to sing about...big things...

(Gesturing to lights operator; in her butchest voice.) – Thank you!

Spotlight comes on. She delivers this number with severe, masculine commitment.

DON'T PUT YOUR FOOT ON A MAN WHEN HE'S DOWN

Society's ways in these curious days

Need much alteration, I'm sure

For seldom you'll see that rich folks agree

With those whom misfortune's made poor.

Now this must be wrong if there's truth in my song,

For a man may be worthy, though poor

Then give him a lift, so he may make shift

To keep off the wolf from his door.

Then I give this advice

Entreating you won't

On your heel turn away with a frown.

When a poor fellow needs it,

Assist him, But don't

Put your foot on a man when he's down.

How many good men have again and again,

Given way 'neath the world's heavy cares?

For want of a start from a generous heart

Whose fortune's been greater than theirs.

And time after time we hear of some crime

Induced by sad poverty, keen,

That might have been stayed, had an effort been made

Before he'd such misery seen.

Then I give this advice

Entreating you won't

On your heel turn away with a frown.

When a poor fellow needs it,

Assist him, but don't

Put your foot on a man when he's down.

(Taking off dinner jacket.) In 1858 Annie Hindle employed an attractive young woman called Miss Ella Wesner as her dresser *(She holds out jacket as if to dresser.)* …Ella was a quick learner, it seems, because by 1860 she was treading the boards herself – *(Slipping the jacket back on.)* in a suit. Tall, broad and handsome, Ella was, it seems, a born trouser-wearer; a New York newspaper commented that *(Back on mike.)* 'With her faultless form, and face quite masculine, Nature has liberally endowed her for her specialty', and quoted a female member of the audience saying admiringly, as Ella stepped on stage – 'You wouldn't know'…

– But of course that lady did know – just as you know

That I know

That you know

That we're all in this act together…

…this next number is your chance to prove that, by joining in; from the 'King Song-book' of Miss Ella Wesner, The Mash Idol, I give you that classic tale of thwarted Trouser-love, 'Down by The Old Mill Stream'

DOWN BY THE OLD MILL STREAM

Piano intro, during which she fetches a farmer's hat. She sings this number in a comedy rural accent.

You must know that my uncle is a farmer,

Keeps a large farm in the West.

'Twas there that I met a little charmer

And many's the time I've caress'd...

The damsel fair with nut brown hair

Her equal ne'er was seen,

And where I met that charmin' little pet

Was down by the old mill stream....

> *She unfurls a sheet with the lyrics of the chorus painted on it,
> and announces:*
>
> – Now there's no need to get tense. I'll be singing the
> first chorus, and then you can be joinin' in next time
> round…

Down by the old mill stream

There, many happy hours I've seen

Strolling day by day the time I passed away

Down by the old mill stream.

Her father was the owner of a dairy

Her brother worked at the plough

And while I would roam with dear Mary

Her mother would go and milk the cow.

Her father said that we should not wed

– Which I thought was rather mean.

As she could not be my wife, she said she'd end her life

By drowning in the old mill stream...

> – I need your help now…

Down by the old mill stream – I can't hear you!

There, many happy hours I've seen

Strolling day by day the time I passed away

Down by the old mill stream... **not bad.**

The old man laughed at his daughter

Saying 'I don't believe a word you say'

But when he saw her struggling In the water

He exclaimed 'Oh save her, pray!'

It was too late – she'd met her fate,

Oh what a dreadful scene.

The old man cried as the neighbours tried

To pull her out of the old mill stream....

Down by the old mill stream – **where's it to, then?**

There, many happy hours I've seen

Strolling day by day the time I passed away

Down by the old mill stream... **respect now.**

At last they got her out of the water

When some of the neighbours said

'Oh, Brown, you've been the ruin of your daughter,

For that girl is really...dead.'

He tore his hair, gave way to despair,

Ran away, never more was seen

And now I'm told that the dairy is sold

That stood by the old mill stream...

> *Blowing nose on handkerchief, and unable to join in first two lines of chorus, she is so overcome by sentiment...*

Down by the old mill stream

There, many happy hours I've seen

Strolling day by day the time I passed away

Down by the old mill stream.

> *(Into mike.)* There you are, you see; not just a sing-a-long; more...a collaboration...

She clears away the song-sheet.

In real life – you'll be pleased to hear – the story ended happily; Ella did get the girl. In 1872 she eloped with a notorious New York actress, Miss Josie Mansfield – and spent the next ten years openly living with her in Paris. It was 1917 when Ella made her last appearance as a man – back in the States, and on Broadway. Her last wish was that she should lie in state in the Campbell Funeral Church, on Broadway and 66th, in her suit, and then be buried in it. Her last wish – and she got it.

Farmer's hat back on stand; she picks up a bowler hat.

(On mike.) Ella and Annie both impersonated **men**; by the time the First World War was over, things got a bit more circumspect – the impersonators developed a decided taste for the boyish. **X** Facial hair was unknown; **X** clothes were sharply cut and tight-fitting **X** ...and the body beneath them was never a threat. **X** Whatever the excuse was, whether the trousers belonged to *(A different pose for each chord.)* a masher **X** a johnny **X** a toff **X** a bank clerk **X** a telegraph boy **X** – even, on occasion, a fresh-faced curate **X!!** ...the alibi was always *immaturity* – no matter how much he talked about ladies. Which was often...often.

The piano plays an upbeat intro under.

Ladies and gentlemen, welcome to the strangely one-track world of the most popular Christian name amongst trousered alter egos...Here's...Johnny!

WHY DID I KISS THAT GIRL

Bashful Johnny Green

Just turned seventeen

Wore his first long pants

When some friends he knew

Introduced him to

Mabel at a dance.

She was awful nice

So he kissed her twice

Then he ran away.

One week later all the gang heard bashful Johnny say...Oh! —

Why did I kiss that girl?

Why, oh why, oh why?

Why did I kiss that girl?

I could almost cry.

I'm nervous, so nervous,

I'm worried and blue

And if her kiss did that

What would her huggin' do?

Ma says that I'm a wreck

I'll admit, she's right

Pa says he'll break my neck

He can't sleep at night.

They're upset and all because

I ain't like I used to wuz

Why did I kiss that girl?

Why, oh why, oh why?

Joe and Jack and Jim

All kept after him

Almost ev'ry day.

'Get her on the phone,

See if she's alone,

You'll win her that way.'

Johnny fell again

He kissed her and then

Ran away once more.

When he saw the gang next day, well, he began to roar...Oh! –

Why did I kiss that girl?

Why, oh why, oh why?

Why did I kiss that girl?

I could almost cry.

I'm nervous, so nervous,

I'm worried and blue

And if her kiss did that

What would her huggin' do?

Ma says that I'm a wreck

I'll admit, she's right

Pa says he'll break my neck

He can't sleep at night.

They're upset – it's plain to see,

They don't like this brand new me

Why did I kiss that girl?

Why, oh why, oh why?

Why, oh why, oh why?

> – Nobody stays seventeen for long...here's Johnny, a year later, up at Oxford, learning to be a *man*...

FOLLOWING IN FATHER'S FOOTSTEPS

To follow in your father's footsteps is a motto for each boy

And following in father's footsteps is a thing I much enjoy

My mother caught me out last evening up the West End on a spree

She said 'Where are you going?'

But I answered 'Don't ask me...'

I'm following in father's footsteps

I'm following the dear old dad.

He's just in front with a fine, big gal,

So I thought I'd have one as well.

I don't know where he's going...

But when he gets there, I'll be glad

I'm following in father's footsteps – yes!

I'm following the dear old dad...

> I say, Pater!

> *The pianist keeps the music going under –*

As Oscar Wilde should have said, *(Getting a cigarette out of a cigarette-case.)* to sing one song about becoming like one's father may be accounted a misfortune, but to sing *two* – well, in a show about male impersonators, I'm afraid it's almost impossible to avoid – I mean where else is a girl to get her ideas about masculine behaviour…so, here's Johnny! – again…

I'M SOWING ALL MY WILD OATS

My dear old father long ago used to say

'Before a boy into a man can grow

His wild oats he is bound to sow'

And, like a good son should, I think father's way

And so before I settle down

I mean to paint the town all red.

The game's rather dear, as the dad's chequebook shows,

But I'm having a real good time, boys,

And I don't care if it snows…

I'm sowing all my wild oats

I'm learning how to be a man

I'm sowing all my wild oats

And stop me no one can

I'm a little bit of hot stuff

What father says is true

I'm sowing all my wild oats… *(Eyeing a woman in the audience.)*

And a bit of someone else's, too…

– I said earlier no one stays young forever...but that doesn't seem to stop the men in these songs from trying. Here's Johnny *several* years later...

She swaps her cigarette for a cigar – clutches an empty bottle – and ages by about thirty years.

HI! WAITER

Lovely woman was made to be loved,

To be fondled and courted and kissed

And all those who've never made love to a girl

Well, they don't know the fun they have missed.

I'm a fellow who's up to the times,

Just the boy for a lark or a spree,

There's a chap that's dead set on the women and wine

You can bet your old boots that it's me –

Hi! Waiter! A dozen more bottles

Let's show the ladies a really good spree

My dad was a banker, so fill 'er up, Jimmy boy,

Hang the expense – put it all down to me.

Trips over.

I'm beginning to think I am tight

But I think I have room for one, yet

I'm afraid that cigar was a little too strong,

So it's back to the old cigarette.

Now, I feel I'm as good as a king,

Come along – share a bottle with me

My eyes magnify – there's but one, I know well,

But of waiters, I see sixty three...

> *Big instrumental build-up to second chorus; crosses to mike, then, suddenly...*

...Just before we move on, I'd like to say that that's an Ella Wesner song; Ella Wesner, who died with her suit on; how strange and how marvellous it must have been for her, to sing those words –

'And all those who've never made love to a girl – well, they don't know the fun they have missed.'

> *Something about that line makes her drift away into a smile…*

Now where was I?

> *The piano prompts her with a chord.*

Ah yes…

Eventually, of course, Johnny does get older. But no matter how decrepit he gets, he's still singing the same old song.…

> *She loses bottle and cigarette, and collects a pipe – she is now an old man.*

I'VE GOT THE TIME, I'VE GOT THE PLACE

I'm blue all through

And I'll tell my troubles all to you.

It's all because I have no girly sweet to cheer me

When my weary heart is dreary.

All alone in my home – I'm about as sad as I can be

I've got the time to spare, the place to share,

But not a girly seems to care for me.

I've got the time, I've got the place,

Will someone kindly introduce me to the girl?

She needn't be so very pretty – I don't care much for a face,

And I don't give a jot if her petticoat and things are trimmed with lace.

She may be tall, she may be small,

She may be any, any, any kind at all quite frankly –

Gee – ain't it kind of funny when a fella's got the money

And the time, and the place,

But it's gosh darn hard to find the girl...

...She may be tall, she may be small,

She may be any, any, any kind at all –

Yes – ain't it kind of funny when a fella's got the money

And the time, and the place,

But it's gosh darn hard to find the girl.

> *She stands disconsolately looking from left to right, as if for a girl. Final swig of drink on end of play-out.*

What must it have been like for a woman to grow old as a young man? To put on trousers to go to work every night of your life? When did the applause begin to grate, I wonder...?

(On mike.) Ella Shields, third of the great British impersonators, performed this next number – her greatest hit, written for her by her husband – for 39 years. Forced, following a divorce from the aforementioned husband, to stage a come-back tour at the age of seventy three, Ella last sang it on the evening of August 3rd, 1952, while performing in a holiday camp in Morecambe Bay. Five minutes after the end of the song, she collapsed on the way to her dressing

room, and died that night. But that's not what people remember about her. What they remember, is this song. Ladies and gentlemen I give you; Miss **X** Ella **X** Shields **X**…

BURLINGTON BERTIE FROM BOW

She collects her top hat and white gloves – then leans against the table during the intro, creating the image of the elderly Ella waiting in the wings.

I'm Bert – p'rhaps you've heard of me

Bert, you've had word of me

Jogging along, hearty and strong,

Living on plates of fresh air.

I dress up in fashion and when I am feeling depressed

I shave from my cuff all the whiskers and fluff,

Put my hat on and toddle up West…

I'm Burlington Bertie, I rise at Ten Thirty

And saunter along like a toff.

I walk down the Strand with my gloves on my hand

Then I walk down again with them off.

I'm all airs and graces – correct easy paces,

Without food so long, I've forgot where my face is

I'm Bert – Bert – I haven't a shirt

But my people are well off, you know.

Nearly everyone knows me, from Smith to Lord Roseb'ry,

I'm Burlington Bertie – from Bow.

I smile condescendingly

While they're extending me

Cheer upon cheer, when I appear

Captain of my polo team.

So strict are my people – they're William the Conqueror's strain,

If they ever knew I'd been talking to you,

Well, they'd never look at me again...

I'm Burlington Bertie, I rise at Ten Thirty

Then saunter along Temple Bar.

As round there I skip, I keep shouting 'Pip, pip!'

And the darn'd fools think I'm in my car.

At Rothchild's I swank it – my body, I plank it

On his front doorstep with *The Mail* for a blanket

I'm Bert – Bert, and Rothchild was hurt

He said, 'You can't sleep there!' I said 'Oh?'

He said 'I'm Rothchild, sonny', I said

'That's damn funny – I'm Burlington Bertie from Bow.'

   Takes monocle from inside jacket pocket.

My pose, though ironical

Shows that my monocle

Holds up my face – keeps it in place,

Stops it from slipping away.

Cigars – I smoke thousands,

I usually deal in the Strand,

But you've got to take care when you're getting them there

Or some idiot will stand on your hand...

> *Stops.*

> – At this point, on the third of August 1952, Ella forgot her words… She stopped, looked at the audience, paused and said

> 'I used to be Burlington Bertie, you know'.

> And then…she carried on.

...I am Burlington Bertie, I rise at Ten Thirty

And Buckingham Palace I view

I stand in the yard while they're changing the guard

And the King shouts across 'Toodle-oo!'

The Prince of Wales' brother – along with some other –

Pats me on the back and says 'Come and see mother'

I'm Bert – Bert – and royalty's hurt

They once asked me to dine, I said 'No!

I've just had a banana with Lady Diana,

I'm Burlington Bertie – from Bow!'

> *She waves, and turns upstage… The music turns into a haunting lament, then stops. She walks slowly back to the mike, laying down the hat and gloves with sadness and respect.*

Ella worked till the bitter end – as did Hetty King – with, in her case, the emphasis definitely on the bitter. Right at the end of her career, at the age of eighty, she was still defending herself against accusations that her work – and therefore she – was unwomanly.

'Some people would ask whether she' – Hetty often referred to herself in the press in the third person –

'was masculine offstage. Oh well, one can't prevent what people think... I did get letters, terrible letters, declaring that they can't eat or sleep or are going to kill themselves for love. Sickening. What can one say? It was all just a performance...'

Thanky you Hetty...

And she wasn't the only one *(Taking the mike off its stand, and beginning to pace the stage.)* In 1930s Harlem the six foot cross-dressing cabaret queen and out bull-dagger Gladys Bentley was as famous for her white satin tuxedo, her matching white topper and her girlfriends as she was for her singing of the blues. But in 1956, Gladys – who at the height of her career had Bea Lillie, Tallulah Bankhead and the young, as-yet unknown Joan Crawford calling round at her Fifth Avenue apartment after the show – was forced to publish a public recantation. Under the headline 'I am a woman again', she detailed how treatment with female hormones had allowed her to turn her back on

'That fantasy world of twinkling bright lights in which some of us dreamed of finding a way of life different from that approved of by society'

And to have

'Found happiness in the prospect of married love at last.'

Well, that may have been what she said in print; what she sang – with some of the most notorious ladies of New York at her magnificent feet...was this...

BABY, WON'T YOU PLEASE COME HOME

I've got the blues – I feel so lonely

I'd give the world if I could only make you understand

That really would be grand.

I'm gonna telephone my baby

Ask her – won't you please come home?

'Cos when she's gone I worry all night long.

Baby, won't you please come home?

Baby, won't you please come home?

I have tried, in vain, never more to call your name.

When you left you broke my heart

That will never make us part.

Every hour of the day you will hear me say

Baby, won't you please come home?...

Stands, takes a drink during instrumental.

...When you left you broke my heart

That will never make us part.

Every hour of the day you will hear me say

Baby, won't you please come home?

Baby, won't you please come home?

She puts the mike back on its stand.

Following the publication of that article, Gladys did get work again – albeit as a novelty act on Groucho Marx's TV variety show – and in a dress. She also did manage to get married, first to a sailor, then to a theatrical columnist...hmmmnnn...well, she wasn't the first, and she won't be the last.

She steps away from the mike.

You'll be pleased to hear that not everyone gave up their trousers to get married... In June 1886, Annie

Hindle tied the knot with her dresser, Miss Annie Ryan – after show, in a hotel room – but in front of a minister. The groom wore a dress suit; the bride a dress – and the best man was a female impersonator. When the news got out, the minister in question was tracked down by a journalist from *The New York Sun*, to whom he gave an interview in which he said –

'I know all the circumstances. The groom gave me her – I mean his – name as Charles Hindle, and he assured me that he was a man. I had no other course to pursue. The bride is a sensible girl, and she is of age. I believe they love each other, and that they will be happy.'

I hope they were. Was it her wife, I wonder, that Annie was privately thinking of, when she stepped out on stage in one of the severely tailored Civil War uniforms that her many female fans so much admired, and sang this…?

With military fervour.

THE GIRL I LEFT BEHIND ME

The hour was sad I left the maid

A lingering farewell taking

Her sighs and tears my steps delayed

I thought her heart was breaking.

In hurried words her name I blessed

I breathed the vows that bind me

And to my heart in anguish pressed

The girl I left behind me.

Then forth I strode to battle fierce

To win a name in story

And there when dawned the sun of day

There dawned our day of glory.

As blazed the noon on mountain's height

Therein the post assigned me

I shared the glory of that fight

Sweet girl I left behind me.

Surrounded now by friends and kin

Who smile, weep and caress me

I watch the tears of joy that fall

As each dear one does kiss me.

But there is one who moves my soul

My tears now almost blind me

God grant I'll be obliged no more

To leave my girl behind me...

...God grant I'll be obliged no more

To leave my girl behind me

> Annie's story has a strange last chapter. So far as we know, she never did leave her girl behind her – but her marriage did cost her her career. Her audience, having read that she'd signed the marriage register as 'Charles', started to think that they'd been fooled – that the she they'd been applauding actually *was* a he, instead of just looking like one – and so…they no longer believed in her act. By appearing as her true self, Annie had become a fraud…

What people wanted from these women, it seems, was not just Glamour...

X

And Skill

X

But also...Illusion...or, as I like to call it; *Possibility.*

X...

I'd like to end the show with perhaps the most famous of these songs, sung by certainly the most famous of these ladies. 'After The Ball' was written by Charles K Harris – the first man to ever earn a million dollars in royalties – and sung by Miss...Vesta...Tilley.

The lights turn midnight blue, and she is caught in a spotlight – a Sickert painting come to life.

AFTER THE BALL

A little maiden climbed an old man's knee

Begged for a story – 'Do, uncle, please!

Why are you single? Why live alone?

Have you no babies? Have you no home?'

I had a sweetheart, years, years ago –

Where she is now, pet, you will soon know

List to the story, I'll tell it all

I believed her faithless after the ball.

After the ball is over

After the break of morn

After the dancers' leaving
After the stars are gone,
Many a heart is aching
If you could read them all
Many the hopes that have vanished
After the ball.

Bright lights were flashing in the grand ballroom
Softly the music playing sweet tunes
There came my sweetheart – my love, my own
'I wish some water – leave me alone.'
When I returned, dear, there stood a man
Kissing my sweetheart as lovers can
Down fell the glass, pet, broken, that's all
Just as my heart was after the ball.

After the ball is over
After the break of morn
After the dancers' leaving
After the stars are gone,
Many a heart is aching
If you could read them all
Many the hopes that have vanished
After the ball.

Long years have passed, child, I never wed

True to my lost love, though she is dead

She tried to tell me – tried to explain

I would not listen; pleadings were vain.

One day a letter came from that man

He was her brother, the letter ran –

That's why I'm lonely, no home at all

I broke her heart, pet, after the ball...

> *Piano chords – a chiming clock – between the next words.*

> Annie... **X** ...Ella... **X** ...Hetty... **X** ...Gladys... **X** ...Vesta... **X** ... and all the others...thank you –

After the ball is over

After the break of morn

After the dancers' leaving

After the stars are gone,

Many a heart is aching

If you could read them all

Many the hopes that have vanished

After the ball.

Thank you, and goodnight.

.

NEIL BARTLETT

Neil Bartlett is a director and author. He was an early member of Complicité (winning the Perrier Award with them for *More Bigger Snacks Now* back in 1985). From 1988 to 1998 he created a series of thirteen works with his company Gloria, including *A Vision of Love Revealed in Sleep*, *Sarrasine* and *Night After Night*. From 1994 to 2005 he was the Artistic Director of the Lyric Hammersmith in London, where he directed thirty-one productions ranging from Shakespeare to pantomime.

His translations of Genet, Kleist, Labiche, Marivaux, Molière and Racine, along with his adaptations of Dickens and Dumas, have been widely performed throughout Britain and North America, including productions at the National, the RSC, the Manchester Royal Exchange, the Goodman Theatre in Chicago and the American Repertory Theater in Boston.

Neil's recent theatre work includes Wilde's *An Ideal Husband* at the Abbey Theatre in Dublin, Shakespeare's *Romeo and Juliet* for the RSC, Britten's *The Turn of the Screw* at Aldeburgh, *Or You Could Kiss Me* at The National Theatre (a collaboration with Handspring Puppet Company), *For Alfonso* for the Brighton Festival, *The Madness of an Extraordinary Plan* (a collaboration with Sir Mark Elder and the Halle Orchestra for the Manchester International Festival) and a new staging of Tchaikovsky's *The Queen of Spades* for Opera North. His most recent novel, *Skin Lane*, was shortlisted for the Costa Prize.

You can find out more about his past and current work at www.neil-bartlett.com.

JESSICA WALKER

Jessica Walker studied at the Guildhall School of Music and Drama, and has performed roles for companies including Opera North, Musiktheater Transparant, Glyndebourne, National Reisopera and The Opera Group.

Her recent concert work has ranged from Ligeti's *Aventures/ Nouvelles Aventures* for Psappha, to *Mercy and Grand: The Tom Waits Project* with Opera North, which toured widely, from Leeds to Milan. A CD from her concert tour, *A Quiet Girl, Songs of Love and other Disasters* is released on the Avid label.

The Girl I Left Behind Me is her first creative collaboration, and has toured to critical acclaim, including performances at the Howard Assembly Room Leeds, Purcell Room London, Sage Gateshead, Brighton Theatre Royal, Aldeburgh Festival, Coutts Arts Festival, Buxton Festival and the Barbican Pit.

Future plans include further performances of *Mercy and Grand* at St George's Hall, Bristol and the Spitalfields Winter Festival (to coincide with its CD release on the Gavin Bryar's label), and her next solo show, *Patricia Kirkwood is Angry*, with the Manchester Royal Exchange and Opera North.

OTHER NEIL BARTLETT TITLES

Original Work Single Editions
Or You Could Kiss Me
£9.99 / 9781849431002

In Extremis
£6.99 / 9781840022056

Collections
Solo Voices: Monologues 1987-2004
£12.99 / 9781840024654

Queer Voices
£14.99 / 9781849431668

Translations & Adaptations
Oliver Twist
Dickens/Bartlett £7.99 / 9781840023602

A Christmas Carol
Dickens/Bartlett £7.99 / 9781840023992

Great Expectations
Dickens/Bartlett £8.99 / 9781840027266

Camille
Dumas/Bartlett £7.99 / 9781840023602

The Island of Slaves
Marivaux/Bartlett £7.99 / 9781840022971

La Casa Azul: Inspired by the writings of Frida Kahlo
Faucher/Bartlett £7.99 / 9781840023480

Marivaux: Two Plays
Marivaux/Bartlett £12.99 / ISBN: 9781840027464

The Prince of Homburg
Von Kleist/Bartlett £7.99 / 9781840022674

The Threesome
Labiche/Bartlett £7.99 / 9781840021554

WWW.OBERONBOOKS.COM

Follow us on www.twitter.com/@oberonbooks
& www.facebook.com/oberonbook

www.ingramcontent.com/pod-product-compliance
Ingram Content Group UK Ltd.
Pitfield, Milton Keynes, MK11 3LW, UK
UKHW020729280225
455688UK00012B/562